MOUNTAINS

A TRUE BOOK

by

Larry Dane Brimner

Children's Press®
A Division of Grolier Publishing
New York London Hong Kong Sydney
Danbury, Connecticut

The Karakoram
Range, Pakistan

Subject Consultant
Peter Goodwin
Science Teacher, Kent School,
Kent, Connecticut

Reading Consultant
Linda Cornwell
Coordinator of School Quality
and Professional Improvement
Indiana State Teachers
Association

Author's Dedication:
To Cheryl Yeatts and my
young friends at West Sedona
Elementary School, for
red rock memories.

The photograph on the cover
shows Mount McKinley in
Alaska. The photograph on
the title page shows the
Dolomite Range in Italy.

**Visit Children's Press® on the
Internet at:
http://publishing.grolier.com**

Library of Congress Cataloging-in-Publication Data

Brimner, Larry Dane
    Mountains / by Larry Dane Brimner.
        p. cm. — (A True book)
    Includes bibliographical references (p.).
    Summary: Describes what mountains are, how they are formed, what
kinds of plants and animals live on them, and how they affect the sur-
rounding weather.
        ISBN 0-516-21568-X (lib. bdg.)   0-516-27192-X (pbk.)
        1. Mountains—Juvenile literature [1. Mountains.] I. Title. II. Series.
GB512.B75 2000
551.43'2—dc21   99-058039
                                                                  CIP
                                                                  AC

GROLIER
PUBLISHING

Contents

Wonders of the Natural World   5

How Mountains Form   12

Wearing Away   24

Mountains and Weather   31

Life on Mountains   37

To Find Out More   44

Important Words   46

Index   47

Meet the Author   48

Mount Rainier in Washington (left) and the Himalayas (below)

Wonders of the Natural World

Mountains are among the most dramatic wonders of the natural world. Some stand as solitary peaks, but most form in long chains called ranges. The highest of these ranges are the Himalayas in Asia.

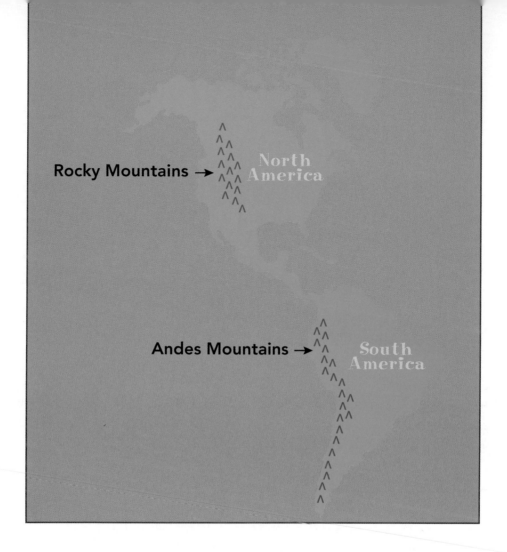

Rocky Mountains → North America

Andes Mountains → South America

Some of the longest ranges, however, are found in the western parts of the Americas. The Rocky Mountains extend from northern Canada to New Mexico in the southern United States. The Andes stretch from one end of South America to the other, a distance of more than 4,500 miles (7,200 kilometers).

The Rocky Mountains in Colorado (right) and the Andes in Chile (below)

The World's

Mount
Everest

K2

Highest Peaks

The Himalayas are the highest mountains in the world above sea level. Believe it or not, they started out on the bed of an ancient ocean. Now, they stretch 1,500 mi. (2,410 km) through southern Asia and have fourteen peaks that stand higher than 26,000 ft. (7,924 m). The two tallest are Mount Everest, at 29,028 ft. (8,848 m); and K2, at 28,250 ft. (8,611 m). North America's tallest peak, by contrast, is Alaska's Mount McKinley, at 20,320 ft. (6,194 m).

Mount McKinley

Mountains are found on every continent. These towering barriers have helped shape the lives of people who live on or near them. They have been natural obstacles to travel, but they have also kept invaders out. They have created deserts, but they also store water and control the flow of rivers.

In spite of all their rugged magnificence, though, mountains are not everlasting. They

Mountains are natural obstacles to human travel.

are born. They grow and change their shapes. And over time, they wear away.

How Mountains Form

Scientists believe the Earth is made up of layers. The outer layer is somewhat like the peel of an orange. We call that thin outer layer the surface. A rocky layer lies beneath the surface. The surface and the rocky layer beneath it make up the Earth's crust.

Mountains are formed by movement of the Earth's plates.

Beneath the crust is a layer of solid rock. This layer and the crust form the lithosphere, the outer shell of the Earth.

The lithosphere is broken into eight major pieces, or plates, and several smaller ones. These plates float on a layer of hot, liquid rock called magma. In some places, the Earth's plates move against each other. In other places, they move apart. They have been in motion for millions of years.

Most of the time the plates move so slowly that people don't notice. But sometimes there is a sudden, sharp

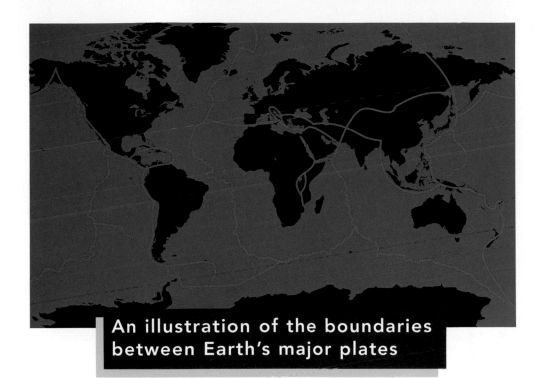

An illustration of the boundaries between Earth's major plates

movement, and we feel the jolt as an earthquake.

Most scientists think that mountains are the result of the slow movements of Earth's plates. Because the plates move in different ways,

Folded mountains, like these in Argentina, form when plates press up against each other.

different kinds of mountains form. Folded mountains form when two plates press against each other. The tremendous pressure causes great waves of rock to lift and fold. This is the process that caused the Himalayas to form.

As Earth's plates have moved, they have made long cracks, or faults, in the Earth's crust. Huge blocks of rock on either side of the faults may push up or slip down, forming fault-block mountains.

A fault in the Earth's crust

Fault-block mountains have a gentle slope on one side and a steep face on the other.

Fault-block mountains—like the Sierra Nevada in North America—usually have a gentle slope on one side and a steep face on the other.

Sometimes magma finds a vent, or opening, in the solid

A dome mountain

rock layer and oozes under Earth's crust. This pushes up the crust to form dome mountains.

Once in a while, magma finds a vent that reaches all the way to the surface. When the magma reaches the surface, it explodes

Kilauea, a volcano in Hawaii

out of the Earth as lava—hot, liquid rock. After that, the lava cools and hardens. More lava explodes out of the vent and then cools and hardens. When huge deposits of lava pile up around a vent, they form a cone-shaped volcanic mountain. These mountains can form singly or in groups.

Under the ocean, where the lithosphere is thinnest, some of the Earth's plates are moving apart. In these places, magma pushes through the space between the plates. When the magma hits the cold ocean water, it cools and becomes solid.

Over time, the magma builds up to form huge underwater mountain ranges. Some of these mountains rise out of the oceans to form islands, such as the

Mauna Kea in Hawaii

Hawaiian Islands in the Pacific
Ocean. If you were to measure
from the ocean floor, the world's
highest mountain would actually
be Hawaii's Mauna Kea, which
rises 13,796 ft. (4,205 m)
above sea level—but 33,675 ft.
(10,264 m) from the ocean floor.

An Island is Born

On November 14, 1963, a fishing crew saw great clouds of steam escaping from the Atlantic Ocean in a spot near Iceland. The water around the steam bubbled and frothed. Was it a sea monster? No. Deep beneath the ocean's surface, lava was gushing out of a fault in the Mid-Atlantic Range, a chain of undersea mountains that stretches along the ocean floor. Within months, a lava cone had risen above the ocean's surface, and in April 1964, lava poured out of the cone's vent to form the island of Surtsey.

Wearing Away

As soon as mountains form, they begin to be worn away by a process called erosion. It usually happens so slowly that we do not notice it. But from one season to another, wind, rain, and ice are hard at work—changing the shapes and appearances of mountains.

These mountains and valleys were shaped by glaciers.

Strong winds carry particles of grit and sand. Like a sand-blaster or sandpaper, these particles help carve and shape mountains. Rain softens surface materials and washes them away. Rainwater also seeps deep into cracks in exposed rock and freezes. When water freezes, it expands—gets bigger—and this causes parts of the mountain to break away from the rest.

In very cold climates, slow-moving rivers of ice called glaciers change the appearances of mountains by grinding away their surfaces.

A glacier grinds away at a mountain's surface as it moves downhill (above). The Matterhorn in Switzerland (right) was shaped by glacial ice.

Glacial ice also gouges out chunks of mountain rock and carries them downhill. In the process, rough, pyramid-shaped peaks called horns may form. Switzerland's Matterhorn is an example of a peak shaped by glacial ice.

When mountain ranges are young, the peaks are sharp and craggy. Older mountain ranges, however, have had more time to erode. They no longer have the sharp peaks we see on the

The Appalachian Mountains (above) and the Himalayas (right)

younger ranges. Compare the Appalachians in eastern North America with the Himalayas in Central Asia. Which do you think are older?

Mountains and Weather

There is an old saying that mountains create their own weather. This is true because mountain weather varies with altitude, or how high something is above sea level. The higher up you go, the cooler it gets. This is why some mountains have snow on them even

Snowcapped mountains in summer

during summer. It is also why the weather in a valley can be completely different from the weather at the top of a nearby mountain.

Mountains are like giant walls that change the way air flows. They force air to rise, and as it rises, it cools. Air contains an invisible gas called water vapor. The cooler the air becomes, the less water vapor it can hold. As air rises over

the mountains and gets
colder, the water vapor turns
into tiny droplets of water
that become clouds, mist,
fog, and rain.

Mountains also affect the
climate, or the general
weather pattern, of areas far
away from them. Winds form
clouds and drop rainfall on
the leading, or windward,
side of mountains. By the
time the clouds reach the
other side—the leeward

The western, windward, side of Washington's Cascade Range is lush and green (top). On the eastern, leeward side of the range lies a much drier valley (bottom).

side—they have dropped their moisture. So leeward slopes tend to be drier. They

The Atacama Desert in Chile is in the rain shadow of mountains.

are said to be "in the rain shadow." Many of the world's great deserts, such as the Atacama Desert in Chile, are in the rain shadows of mountains.

Life on Mountains

Mountains are one of Earth's biomes, or natural communities. They provide shelter and food for an amazing variety of plants and animals. Although mountain life varies from place to place, it usually follows a pattern determined by available water, altitude, and temperature.

The lower slopes of mountains often have trees and shrubs that shed their leaves in colder weather. Higher up, where it is colder still, there is a zone of cone-bearing trees, such as pines and spruce.

You may have noticed that on some mountains, trees do not grow at all above a certain point. The point at which they stop growing is called the timber line. This is where conditions become too cold for trees

The lower slopes of mountains often have trees that shed their leaves in winter. Higher up is a zone of cone-bearing trees that stay green all year (left). Only mosses, lichens, and hardy grasses can survive the severe climate above the timber line (below).

to survive. Only mosses, lichens, and hardy grasses can grow beyond the timber line.

Many different kinds of animals share the mountains, mostly on the lower slopes. Because conditions can be harsh, some of them have developed special abilities to help them survive.

Mountain goats, for example, are skilled climbers. Even on sheer slopes, they can search for food. Some animals protect themselves from winter weather by hibernating (sleeping through the winter), migrating (traveling to a

(Clockwise from top right): Mountain goats, mountain lions, pikas, llamas, and bighorn sheep are among the animals that have adapted to life in the mountains.

warmer place), or growing thick coats of fur.

People, too, live on the mountains of the world. They

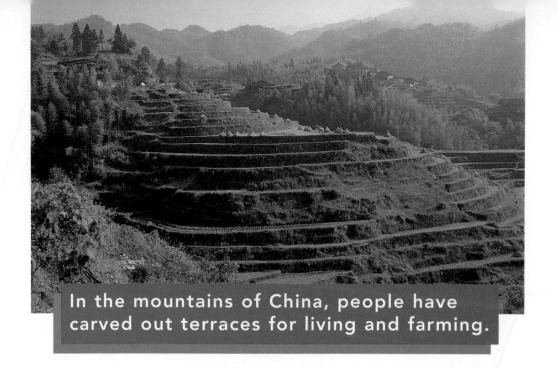

In the mountains of China, people have carved out terraces for living and farming.

carve out terraces for living and farming. They mine valuable minerals with huge earth-moving equipment. They play on ski trails and hiking paths.

But in many places, human activity threatens the very things that people enjoy most about

People skiing
down a
mountainside
in France

mountains—their scenic beauty
and their variety of animal and
plant life. The rugged appear-
ance of these towering barriers is
misleading. People need to treat
mountains with care because
they are as fragile as any of
Earth's other natural homes.

To Find Out More

Here are some additional resources to help you learn more about mountains:

Books

Bramwell, Martyn. **Mountains.** Franklin Watts, 1994.

Collard, Sneed B., III. **Our Natural Homes.** Charlesbridge Publishing, 1996.

Cumming, David. **Mountains.** Thomson Learning, 1995.

Simon, Seymour. **Mountains.** Morrow Junior Books, 1994.

Zoehfeld, Kathleen Weidner. **How Mountains Are Made.** HarperCollins Publishers, 1995.

Organizations and Online Sites

Canadian Rockies Panoramas

http://GeoImages.Berkeley. EDU/GeoImages/QTVR/ CanadianRockies/Canadian Rockies.html

Amazing virtual-reality images of this beautiful mountain range.

Himalayan Portraits

http://aleph0.clarku.edu:80/ rajs/mountain.html

This site includes a clickable range of the Himalayas, photographs and paintings of famous Himalayan mountains, and a list of the world's highest mountains.

Mountain Gallery

http://HTTP.CS.Berkeley. EDU/~qtluong/gallery/ index.html

More than 350 photos of mountains in Europe and North America.

NOVA'S Everest/Earth, Wind, and Ice

http://www.pbs.org/wgbh/ nova/everest/earth/

This in-depth site about Mount Everest includes information about historic expeditions, as well as a geological history of the Himalayas.

Important Words

barrier something that blocks the way or stops movement

continent one of the major land areas of Earth

everlasting lasting forever

leeward on the side sheltered from wind

lichens mosslike plant that grows in patches on rocks or trees

moisture wetness

moss tiny, delicate plant that grows in clumps on rocks or trees

obstacle something that stands in the way

particles very tiny pieces

solitary alone

terraces series of raised, level spaces on a hill or mountain

windward the side the wind strikes

Index

(**Boldface** page numbers indicate illustrations.)

Andes Mountains, **6,** 7, **7**
animals, 40
Appalachian Mountains, 30, **30**
Atacama Desert, 36, **36**
biomes, 37
clouds, 34
deserts, 10
dome mountains, 19, **19**
Earth's crust, 12, 17, 19
Earth's plates, 14, 15, **15,** 16, 21
erosion, 24, 29
fault-block mountains, 17, 18, **18**
faults, 17, **17**
folded mountains, 16, **16**
glaciers, **25,** 27, **28**
Hawaiian Islands, 22
Himalaya Mountains, **4,** 5, **8,** 9, 16, 30, **30**
horn, 29
K2, **8,** 9
lava, 20
leeward side of mountain, 34, 35, **35**

lichens, 39
lithosphere, 13, 14, 21
magma, 14, 18, 19, 21
Matterhorn, **28,** 29
Mauna Kea, 22, **22**
Mid-Atlantic Range, 23
mosses, 39
Mount Everest, **8,** 9
Mount McKinley, **cover,** 9, **9**
mountain goats, 40
Mount Rainier, **4**
rain, 24, 26, **26,** 34
Rocky Mountains, 6, **6,** 7, **7**
Sierra Nevada, 18
snow, 31
Surtsey, 23, **23**
timber line, 38, 39, **39**
underwater mountain ranges, 21
valleys, **25,** 32
vent, 18, 20
volcanic mountains, **20,** 21, **22, 23**
weather, 31
wind, 24, 26
windward side of mountain, 34

Meet the Author

Larry Dane Brimner has written many award-winning books for children, including *Merry Christmas, Old Armadillo* (Boyds Mills Press), *Country Bear's Good Neighbor* (Orchard Books), and *Snowboarding* (Franklin Watts). Among his many titles for Children's Press are *The World Wide Web, Butterflies and Moths,* and *Cockroaches.* When he isn't writing at his desk in San Diego, California, he can usually be found biking in Colorado's Rocky Mountains.

School Dist. 64
164 S. Prospect Ave.
Park Ridge, IL 60068